JOHAN & THE WHALE

STORY & PICTURES BY
— a. simioni —

To my dad.

For everything, but especially for instilling the importance of nature in my heart.

P.S. Snakes still shouldn't be able to swim.

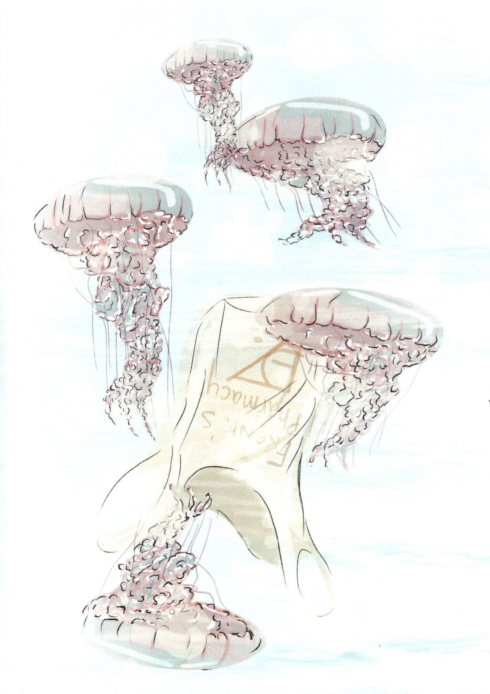

Johan and the Whale

Copyright @ 2022
A. Simioni

YGTMedia Co. Press Trade Paperback Edition

Published in Canada, for Global Distribution by YGTMedia Co.

www.ygtmedia.co/publishing

978-1-989716 75-5

All Rights Reserved. No part of this book can be scanned, distributed, or copied without permission. This book or any portion thereof may not be reproduced or used in any manner whatsoever without the express written permission of the publisher at publishing@ygtmedia.co —except for the use of brief quotations in a book review.

Printed in North America

This is Johan.

He's about nine and lives in a place where the sun always shines.

He loves to play songs on his new ukulele, interrupting his Oma and her quiet time daily.

Today she scoots him out the front door,

"Johan, go to the beach while I wash up these floors.

You can play all your songs to the fish in the sea,

I am sure they will love it, now go, let me be."

You see . . .

Oma's home is near the water,
the beaches and sand,

but Johan never gets wet,
he's always on land.

Until today . . .

At first Johan creates a castle with towers, complete with hand-built tassels and flowers.

He hauls it all home in his little orange crate, hoping his Oma will tell him it's great.

Instead, she's upset with the sand and the dirt,
she only sees mess and piles of work.

Johan and cat head back to the shore,
he probably shouldn't build castles,
but he still can explore!

Johan slips on his flippers
and blue goggles too,

and for the very first time,
he wades into that ocean so blue.

It is salty and warm, much to his surprise,
then a glimmer of light to the right catches his eyes.

A teensy pink sea star is stuck in a cup,
So Johan carefully lifts her up . . . up . . . up . . . up.

Into the sun, then onto the sand,
The starfish goes firm in the palm of his hand.

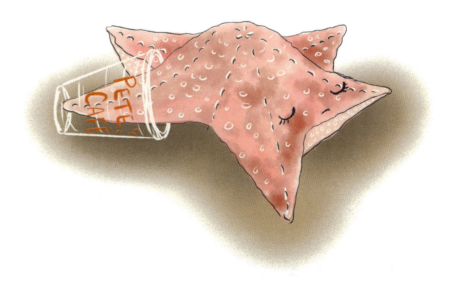

He carries her home
in his towel so plush,

so sweet and cute,
he knows Oma will gush!

"Oma!" Johan calls, but the house is quite empty,
aside the orange fish who always looks grumpy.

An idea comes quickly, filling his head,

The starfish needs an ocean or else she'll be . . .
well you know . . . quite unwell . . . so . . .

Johan and cat fill up the tub to the brim with cool water and eight pounds of salt. It splashes over the edge and onto the floor, soaking through rugs and under the door.

It is then that dear Oma arrives back at home, regretting the choice to leave Johan alone.

"Oh, my word!" Oma hollers. "Look at the floor! This is worse than the sand that you brought home before!"

Johan points her gaze to the star in the bath,
Oma softens a lot and lets out a laugh.

"You poor little critter, stuck in this mess.
When will they learn to not be so careless?"

Oma loosens the cup, they recycle it rightly,
"Now back to the sea!" Oma says brightly.

Johan carries it back to the warm sandy shores,
letting her loose near the dock when he sees so much more.

Two other children found turtles you see,
all stuck in plastic, how could that be?

He knows exactly, precisely,
what they should do,

So the three helping children
head for Oma's home too.

On the doorstep she stands, arms folded and cross,
but again her heart melts when she examines the loss.

They carefully cut loose each bit of trash,
while laying the turtles down in the grass.

As the turtles run free back to the sea,
the children see something they never had seen.

On the dry sandy beach, flapping its tail is none other than a baby gray-and-white whale.

How did a baby gray whale end up here?
Then they see the thing, the thing they all fear.

In the sunshine it glimmers, a sparkling plastic,
The children know they must do something drastic!

They need to get her back to the ocean,
To set her free and end this commotion!

The children surround the whale, gray and white, lifting her up together, with all their strength, all their might.

One . . . two . . . three!

They all tug and up comes the whale,
the littlest children carrying the tail.

Off back to Oma's is the only good choice,
Once she fixes her up, they all can rejoice!

Oma's eyes grow wide as she notices the trail
of thirteen good children carrying a whale!

"Something's stuck in the blowhole," together they call,
So Oma grabs a few tools, her spoon and an awl.

The group heft the whale back to the sea,
They'll unstick the plastic, and they'll set her off free.

Oma hands Johan her good wooden spoon,
"This is your time to shine. You know what to do."

Johan goes to the whale, then climbs to the top,
He is nervous, hands sweaty, he wants to stop.

The gray-and-white whale sits silent and still,
while Johan clears the tape from its tiny blowhole.

At last it is loose, the tape is unstuck!
Oh, what a joy! Oh, what great luck!

The children all cheer as Johan slides his way down,
back to the sandy beach and onto the ground.

They gather around the whale one last time,
sliding her into the water, trusting all will be fine.

As they watch the whale jump with joy and delight,
they realize their beach is a terrible sight.

Old cans, jars, and bags are strewn around,
Through the sand, in the trees, in the grass, on the ground.

Together they collect the trash on the shore,
placing it in bins, like people should have before.

They paint and plant a sign bold and green,
"Put your trash in its place! Please keep it clean!"

And . . .

From that day forth when Johan goes to the shore,
he brings his ukulele like he should have before.

But before he strums all those tunes from Hawaii,
he makes sure the beach is Oma-approved tidy.

A. Simioni, affectionately known as Ella, lives in Toronto, Canada.

You'll generally find her either being cozy at home with her three children, three cats, turtle, hamster, and husband, or collecting odd bits and bobs on the shores of Lake Ontario.

When she's not drawing or painting, she's building fairy gardens, designing handmade rabbits, and crafting with her kids.

Her dad nicknamed her "a little printing press" and taught her everything she knows about the environment.

Manufactured by Amazon.ca
Bolton, ON